W9-AMA-590

DIRT BIKES

MOTORCYCLE MANIA

David and Patricia Armentrout

www.rourkepublishing.com

PHOTO CREDITS: Cover ©Getty Images; pp. 18, 19 ©National Geographic/Getty Images; pp. 7, 10, 11, 13, 17, 21 ©Honda; title page, pp. 4, 5, 9, 15, 22 ©Suzuki

Title page: *Some riders seem to spend more time in the air than on the ground.*

Editor: Frank Sloan

Cover and page design by Nicola Stratford

Library of Congress Cataloging-in-Publication Data

Armentrout, David, 1962-
  Dirt bikes / David and Patricia Armentrout.
    p. cm. -- (Motorcycle mania)
  Includes index.
  ISBN 1-59515-453-1 (hardcover)
  1. Trail bikes--Juvenile literature. I. Armentrout, Patricia, 1960- II.
Title. III. Series.
  TL441.A74 2006
  629.227'5--dc22
                          2005010411

Printed in the USA

CG/CG

Rourke Publishing
1-800-394-7055
www.rourkepublishing.com
sales@rourkepublishing.com
Post Office Box 3328, Vero Beach, FL 32964

TABLE OF CONTENTS

Motorcycles built for off-road riding are often called dirt bikes. They are lighter and easier to handle than their street-legal cousins.

Dirt bikes are built to handle rough trail riding.

Dirt bikes go where no other motorcycles dare.

Dirt bikes don't have fancy accessories or big, comfortable seats. One thing is for sure: Dirt bikes are built for fun!

DIRT BIKES

Dirt bikes are well-designed machines built for a specific purpose—they are not just stripped down versions of road bikes. Some are designed for racing, while others are designed for trail riding. Most dirt bikes, however, are not legal for street use.

Street legal motorcycles must have equipment such as lights, mirrors, turn signals, and a state-issued license or tag.

Fat, knobby tires are perfect for off-road riding.

MORE POWER OR LESS?

Dirt bikes are classified by the size of their engines. The bigger the engine, the more power it has. Bigger engines, however, are not always better. Some riders choose bikes with smaller engines. They are lighter and can be easier to control on jumps and curves.

Dirt bike engines are measured in **cubic centimeters**, or ccs. Standard engine sizes include 50cc, 125cc, 250cc, and 500cc.

Young riders gain experience riding 50cc bikes.

TOUGH MACHINES

Full-size dirt bikes weigh less than 220 pounds (100 kilograms). But they have to be strong to handle the abuse of rough trails. Special **suspension** systems soak up the bumps, so the rider doesn't have to.

Riders love to learn tricks and get "air" off big jumps.

Riders shift their weight in order to maintain control on bumpy terrain.

Knobby tires grab the trail and provide traction in slippery mud. Powerful engines have to be quick and dependable, even after being submerged in water or covered in several inches of mud.

ENDUROS

If you plan to be a dirt bike racer, enduro racing is a great place to get started. Enduros can be long and challenging. Enduro races test the rider's skill and endurance. Races range from a few miles to 150 miles (241 kilometers) long. An Enduro course takes riders through woods, across streams, and over dusty trails.

Riders are judged on their ability to maintain measured speeds over rough terrain. Enduro bikes are dirt bikes, but unlike most off-road motorcycles, they must be street legal.

No matter what kind of motorcycle you ride, it is important to wear proper safety gear such as an approved helmet and tough boots.

Enduro racers must keep a steady pace as they tackle difficult terrain.

MOTOCROSS

Motocross is cross-country motorcycle racing. Motocross races are held on natural terrain tracks that are usually 2 to 2.5 miles (3.2 to 4 kilometers) long. Riders power over steep hills, sharp turns, muddy pits, and nasty bumps on their way around the track. Motocross is the most popular type of **amateur** motorcycle racing.

Dirt bike racers must wear full-faced helmets and body armor to protect themselves in an accident.

Motocross tracks are made up of hills, jumps, and tight turns.

SUPERCROSS

Supercross is similar to motocross, but the races are held inside on man-made tracks. The track is shorter, ranging from 1 to 2 miles (1.6 to 3.2 kilometers) long. Racetrack designers use up to 800 tons of dirt to build steep, gut-wrenching jumps, **berms,** and stutter bumps called **whoops.** Skill isn't enough to get riders through these amazing courses. It also takes a lot of nerve.

Football stadiums, large arenas, and domes are the only places large enough for supercross events.

A lightweight frame and heavy-duty suspension give a racer an advantage on a tight indoor course.

Dirt bikes are not just for racing. They are used for work, too. Some roads and trails are too rough for cars or trucks. Sometimes there are no roads or trails at all. This is when dirt bikes and their riders are most at home.

Dirt bikes are used by cowboys to round up cattle and by rangers to monitor forests. Loggers, miners, hunters, and many others use dirt bikes wherever ordinary vehicles just can't make it.

Horses, dogs, and dirt bikes are ranchers' best friends.

RIDING SAFETY

Safety should come first in action sports. Just as football players wear helmets and body pads for protection, dirt bike riders and racers should wear proper clothing and safety gear to prevent injuries.

A full-faced helmet is the most important piece of safety equipment. Helmets must meet minimum safety standards set by the Department of Transportation (DOT). Many racing organizations also require that helmets be certified by the Snell Memorial Foundation or the American National Standards Institute (ANSI). Riders should also wear goggles, padded gloves, riding pants and jersey, and leather riding boots.

Many riders and racers wear extra protection called body armor. Unlike the medieval style, this armor is made of hard plastic and foam rubber. Body armor protects the shoulders, elbows, chest, and back.

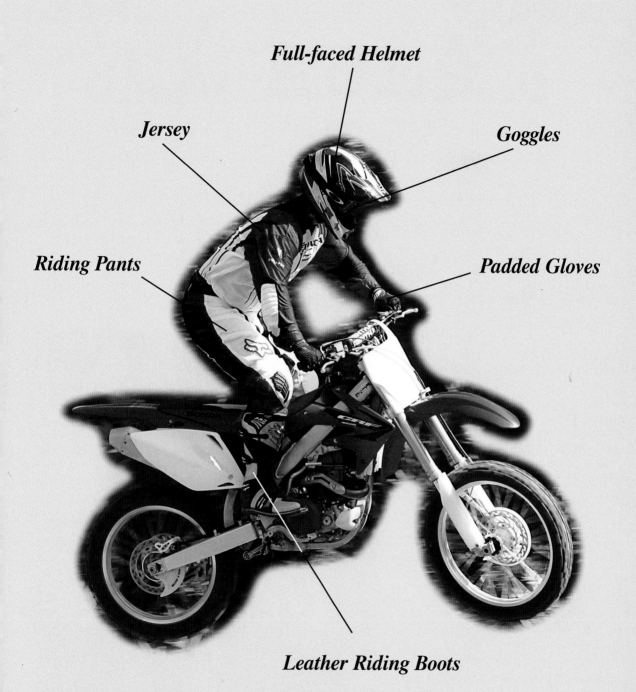

Full-faced Helmet

Goggles

Jersey

Riding Pants

Padded Gloves

Leather Riding Boots

JUST FOR THE FUN OF IT

Not all riders want to race dirt bikes or plan to use one on the job. In fact, most dirt bike owners use their bikes for nothing more than fun rides on their favorite off-road trails. Whatever the reason, dirt bike riders have one thing in common—the thrill of riding a powerful bike that has almost no limits.

This young rider is equipped with all the proper clothing, including a helmet and good fitting gloves and boots.

GLOSSARY

amateur (AM uh tur) — someone who participates in a sport for pleasure rather than money

berms (BERMZ) — banked turns on a motocross or supercross course

cubic centimeters (KYU bik SENT uh mee turz) — the size of the engine cyclinder

motocross (MO TO KROS) — cross-country motorcycle racing

suspension (suh SPEN shun) — the system that cushions the motorcycle from dips and bumps on the course

whoops (HWOOPS) — closely spaced bumps on a motocross or supercross course

INDEX

FURTHER READING

Doeden, Matt. *Dirt Bikes*. Blazers, 2004.
Schwartz, Tina. *Motocross Freestyle*. Capstone Press, 2004.
Seivert, Terri. *Dirt Bike History*. Capstone Press, 2004.

WEBSITES TO VISIT

American Motorcyclist Association
   www.ama-cycle.org/
Off-Road.com
   www.off-road.com/dirtbike/
All Motocross All the Time
   www.motocross.com/

ABOUT THE AUTHORS

David and Patricia Armentrout specialize in writing nonfiction books for young readers. They have had several books published for primary school reading. The Armentrouts live in Cincinnati, Ohio, with their two children.